The Wisdom Our Children Carry

It Opens When We Recognize Our Gifts

Tyrese Gould Jacinto

Dedication

For our children,

who carry wisdom before words were given for it,

who are asked to bend but still remember

how to see, how to feel, how to know.

For those who are misread, misnamed,

and measured by systems too small to hold them.

For our ancestors, who keep the fire, keep the memory,

keep the way of relationship with life and the Creator.

And for our people, who remain present,

who remain heard, who remain enduring.

We are still here.

Table of Contents

Table of Contents

Author's Note

This book was not written to prove that our children are worthy. They have always been worthy. This book was written because too many of our children have been misunderstood by systems that were never designed to see them clearly.

Across generations, many of our families have watched children be judged too quickly. We have seen thoughtful children called slow, sensitive children called distracted, active children called disruptive, and deeply observant children treated as though their gifts had no place in education. We have seen children expected to memorize before they understand, respond before they are ready, and conform before they are known.

These pages come as much from lived experience as from research. They come from family life, from watching children learn in ways that schools often fail to recognize, and from seeing how much damage can be done when difference is treated as deficiency. They also come from love: love for our children, love for our people, and love for ways of knowing that remain rooted in relationship, meaning, and the Creator.

This book is not a claim to speak for all Indigenous peoples of Turtle Island in exactly the same way. No single book could do that. But there are patterns of learning, perception, and understanding that many of our families know intimately, even when institutions do not. This book is an effort to name those patterns with honesty, care, and respect.

It is also an effort to say something simple and necessary: our children are not broken. Many of them are learning in ways that are whole, relational, sensory, reflective, and deeply intelligent. If schools cannot recognize that, then schools must change.

The hope is that this book will help parents feel seen, help educators think more deeply, and help the wider public understand that the issue is not whether our children can learn. The issue is whether they are being taught in ways that honor life, meaning, and relationship.

This work also comes from a deeper need: to address erasure.

For too long, our people have been spoken about as though we belong only to the past.

Too often, our children do not see themselves named, reflected in, or recognized by the stories, teachings, and educational systems around them. Too often, others speak of Indigenous life in ways that remove the living presence of our people from the present moment.

The children's books and spiritual books connected to this work are part of the effort to answer that erasure. They seek to put a name to what has been left nameless, a face to what has been made faceless, and a living presence where absence has too often been assumed. They are meant to help bridge the distance between past and present, so that readers can understand that our people are not merely historical. We are still here.

This matters not only for representation, but for truth. When our children see themselves reflected with dignity, beauty, intelligence, and spirit, something is restored. When others encounter our people through living stories rather than stereotypes, something false begins to loosen. In this way, the work of writing is not separate from the work of healing, remembering, and continuing.

This book serves that same purpose: to help make visible what has too often been overlooked and to affirm that our people remain present, whole, and worthy of being seen.

If these pages help even one child be understood more clearly, help one family feel less alone, or help one teacher slow down long enough to see what a child is truly showing, then this work will have served its purpose.

It is offered in that spirit.

Language Note

In this book, I use the phrases "Indigenous peoples of Turtle Island" and "our people" intentionally.

I do this because many common labels were created through colonial systems and do not always reflect how we understand ourselves. While some of those terms may still appear in research, public institutions, or historical references, they are not always the most respectful or accurate language for a work rooted in lived experience, memory, spirit, and belonging.

The phrase "Indigenous peoples of Turtle Island" helps name the original peoples of this land without relying entirely on colonial geography. The phrase "our people" carries something even deeper. It is relational. It is how many of us speak of ourselves with warmth, kinship, continuity, and recognition. It reminds the reader that we are not a vanished people, not a category, and not a theory. We are living people with memory, intelligence, responsibility, and an enduring connection to the land.

Whenever possible, this book chooses language that honors our presence, our humanity, and our way of knowing.

Introduction

This book examines the learning styles of Indigenous peoples of Turtle Island through both published research and lived experience. It responds to a long-standing educational problem: our children are often misunderstood in classrooms shaped by standardization, speed, memorization, and narrow definitions of intelligence. Across generations, many of our families have observed that these children are not slow learners, but thorough learners. They often seek to understand the whole before the parts, the purpose before the task, and the relationships behind a concept before they can retain it meaningfully.

This distinction matters. When schools reward quick recall, verbal speed, and compliance with rigid classroom routines, our learners may be mislabeled as inattentive, delayed, oppositional, or deficient. Yet research has repeatedly suggested that many of our students demonstrate strengths in holistic, observational, reflective, cooperative, and context-rich learning environments. The literature also points to the importance of family, culture, place, and community in shaping how learning is experienced and remembered.

This book also argues that the issue cannot be understood only through academic categories. For many of our families, learning is inseparable from relationship: relationship to land, animals, elders, story, responsibility, and the Creator. Knowledge is not merely information to be stored. It is something lived, observed, felt, practiced, and carried with respect. This broader way of knowing has often been erased or flattened within the so-called melting pot of American schooling, where Indigenous identities and educational needs have too often been treated as invisible.

The purpose of this book is to bring together scientific literature, Indigenous-centered educational writing, and personal narrative to examine how our people's learning styles are described, where mainstream schooling fails, and what educators and families can do differently. It also draws attention to the public resource developed by the author, "What Is Your Learning Style?"

How This Book Was Gathered

This book uses an integrative review approach combined with personal narrative and reflective analysis. Its sources include public educational materials, peer-reviewed scholarship, Indigenous education resources, and historical and cultural texts provided by the author. The method is qualitative and interpretive rather than experimental.

The review focuses on recurring themes in research on Indigenous peoples of Turtle Island, including holistic and field-dependent learning, observational and demonstration-based learning, reflective response patterns and extended wait time, cooperative rather than competitive classroom preferences, place-based and all-senses experiential learning, and the role of family, elders, culture, and spirituality in meaning-making.

In addition to published literature, this book includes autoethnographic elements drawn from multigenerational family experience. These narratives are not presented as universal claims about all our people. Rather, they are offered as grounded examples of how educational patterns described in the literature may appear in lived family and community life.

This approach has limitations. Research on our people's learning styles is uneven, and some older studies risk overgeneralization when read out of context. At the same time, the relative scarcity of research is itself part of the problem. Our people's learning styles have often been underrepresented, misrepresented, or absorbed into broader educational categories that obscure Indigenous ways of knowing. For that reason, this book treats both the presence and absence of research as meaningful.

What the Research Shows

A substantial body of educational writing describes the learning styles of Indigenous peoples of Turtle Island as tending toward holistic, relational, and observational learning. Pewewardy's review of the literature, widely cited in discussions of Indigenous education, argues that Indigenous students are often better served by instructional approaches that emphasize visualization, reflection, cooperation, and holistic creativity rather than purely linear, competitive, and decontextualized instruction.

A Native Financial Cents educational resource summarizes similar themes, noting that social and affective emphasis, harmony, holistic perspectives, creativity, and nonverbal communication often characterize the learning of our students. It further suggests that many of our people may be more comfortable in field-dependent learning environments, where the whole context matters, and relationships guide understanding. This aligns closely with the central claim of this book: many of our people need to know how, why, and for what purpose something exists before they can meaningfully remember it.

Research-informed teaching guidance from the University of Denver similarly emphasizes place-based learning, storytelling, and all-senses experiential learning. That guidance describes Indigenous learning as rooted in cultural, historical, environmental, and community context. It also cites work suggesting that Indigenous teaching and learning engage the senses of sight, hearing, taste, touch, and smell, as well as intuition and gut feeling.

This is especially important because mainstream classrooms often privilege verbal instruction, sedentary routines, and abstract tasks detached from lived experience.

Another recurring theme in the research is reflectivity. Our students are often described as taking more time to observe, listen, and consider before responding. In classroom settings, this can be misread as hesitation, lack of knowledge, or disengagement. Yet some educational sources argue that this reflectivity reflects care, accuracy, and a desire to understand all sides before speaking. Such a pattern supports the author's observation that silence may not mean disagreement or inability, but a process of careful internal evaluation.

The literature also critiques the mismatch between our learners and conventional schooling. Standard classroom models often reward speed, competition, immediate verbal participation, and fragmented memorization. By contrast, Indigenous-centered educational writing frequently emphasizes demonstration, supervised participation, storytelling, cooperation, and learning through observation. In this framework, knowledge is relational and embodied, not merely verbal.

A broader strand of scholarship in the Journal of American Indian Education has also stressed the role of culture, community, language, and culturally grounded education in academic success. Articles on place-based education, culturally responsive curriculum, valid assessment, and the role of culture in culturally compatible education suggest that outcomes improve when our students are taught in ways that honor identity and lived context rather than forcing assimilation into a single norm.

Emerging from this literature is a consistent conclusion: the problem is not simply whether our people can adapt to school, but whether schools are willing to adapt to our students.

What Emerges From Research and Experience

When the research is read alongside lived experience, several themes emerge with striking consistency. What appears in educational literature is not separate from what many of our families have long observed in daily life. Again and again, the same patterns come into view. Our learners are often described as holistic rather than fragmented, needing to understand the whole before the parts can fully make sense. Observation, modeling, and demonstration remain central to learning. At the same time, reflection and delayed response may indicate depth of processing rather than deficiency. Storytelling and cultural context strengthen memory and meaning. Place, land, and sensory experience shape how knowledge is formed, and family, elders, and community relationships remain educational assets rather than peripheral influences. At the same time, standardized, competitive, and overly verbal classroom models may place our students at a disadvantage.

Taken together, these patterns suggest that our people's learning styles should not be framed as weaknesses or departures from some educational norm. They reflect a coherent educational orientation that has too often been misunderstood within dominant schooling systems. Just as importantly, they show that the distance between research and lived experience is not as wide as institutions sometimes assume. In many cases, the literature is only beginning to describe what families have already known through observation, care, and long experience with their children.

The next section turns more fully to that lived experience, where these patterns can be seen not only as research findings, but as realities carried in homes, relationships, bodies, memory, and the daily lives of our children.

Lived Experience

Learning Through Relationship, Observation, and the Whole

For many of our people, learning does not begin with isolated facts. It begins with relationship. A child may first need to feel safe with the person teaching, understand the purpose of what is being shown, and sense how that knowledge connects to life as a whole. Without that connection, information may seem empty, difficult to hold, or unworthy of memory. This does not reflect a lack of intelligence. It reflects a different order of understanding.

In many families, children are taught first by watching. They observe tone, movement, timing, expression, and consequence before they are expected to perform a task themselves. They may listen quietly for a long time, appearing passive to those who do not understand this way of learning. Yet inwardly, they are studying everything. They are gathering the whole picture before acting. When they finally move, speak, or try, it is often with more depth than others expected.

This pattern can be misunderstood in classrooms shaped by speed. A child who does not answer immediately may be seen as unsure. A child who looks away while listening may be judged inattentive. A child who needs to move, touch, or experience something directly may be labeled disruptive. But for many of our people, observation is participation. Silence is thought. Movement is part of concentration. Sensory contact is part of memory.

A Family Pattern Misread by Schooling

Across generations, many families have seen the same pattern. Children who were deeply perceptive, imaginative, and careful were often treated as if they were behind. In truth, they were often trying to understand more than what the lesson allowed. They were not merely repeating an answer. They were trying to understand why the answer mattered, how it fit into life, and whether it carried truth.

Within my own family, this pattern has been clearly evident. What schools may call slow processing is often a form of thorough processing. A child may need to see the whole before accepting the part. They may need to feel the meaning of a lesson before memorizing its surface. They may become tired in environments filled with too many words, too much sitting, bright colors, clutter, pressure, or noise. Their minds are not empty in those moments. They are often over-processing, over-sensing, or trying to organize too many layers at once.

This kind of learner may struggle in settings that demand constant verbal output, yet thrive when given demonstrations, stories, real examples, nature, rhythm, and time. Such learners may remember what they have lived far better than what they have been told. They may understand through sound, image, movement, or feeling before they can explain something in formal academic language.

The Child Who Sees More Than the Lesson

One of the deepest failures of modern schooling is that it often measures only the narrow slice of intelligence it knows how to reward. A child may be highly aware of animals, weather, emotional tone, land, or the suffering of living things, yet receive no recognition for those forms of perception. A child may communicate deeply with nature, notice patterns others miss, or respond strongly to what a place carries, and still be treated as though such awareness has no educational value.

Yet in many Indigenous ways of knowing, these forms of awareness are not meaningless. They are part of life itself. They help shape responsibility, sensitivity, and understanding. A child who notices the distress of animals or the condition of trees is not distracted from learning. That child may already be learning at a profound level.

This matters because many of our children are judged by systems that do not recognize the full range of human perception. When schools ignore intuitive, sensory, relational, and land-based forms of knowing, they do not simply fail to teach well; they fail to teach at all. They teach children to distrust themselves.

Learning With the Body, the Senses, and the Land

For many of our people, learning is not only mental. It is bodily. It may involve walking, touching, tasting, building, hearing, repeating, and being present in the natural world. Some children understand best when they can move. Others need to handle materials, hear the rhythm of words, or connect ideas to outdoor experience. Some become exhausted by long periods of stillness and abstraction, not because they are incapable, but because the method itself runs counter to how their minds and bodies gather meaning.

This is one reason many of our learners do well with stories, examples, and lived demonstrations. A story carries emotion, sequence, memory, and purpose all at once. A demonstration shows not only what to do, but when, why, and with what attitude. Time on the land teaches interdependence, patience, observation, and consequence in ways no worksheet can fully replace.

When education is separated from the senses, from movement, and from the living world, many children are forced to learn in fragments. But for our people, knowledge often arrives as a whole experience.

Spiritual Understanding and the Meaning of Knowledge

For many of our people, learning also carries spiritual meaning. This does not necessarily mean formal ritual. It means that life itself is understood as connected. The land, the animals, the people, the elements, and the Creator are not separate categories. They are part of one living reality. In that understanding, knowledge is not just for testing. It is for right relationship.

This has deep educational implications. A child may resist learning that feels empty, disconnected, or harmful. They may respond more deeply when knowledge is tied to care, truth, usefulness, beauty, or responsibility. They may need to know not only how something works, but whether it serves life.

This way of learning is often invisible in mainstream education because schools are trained to separate intellect from spirit, fact from meaning, and achievement from responsibility. But many of our families know that children learn best when knowledge is alive, purposeful, and connected to the whole of existence.

Toward the Next Section

The lived experiences described here do not stand apart from the literature. They give it flesh. They show how educational patterns become real in homes, families, bodies, and memory. In the next section, this book turns more directly to the ways schools misread our children and how those misreadings can shape identity, confidence, and possibility across generations.

How Schools Misread Our Children

When Difference Is Treated as Deficiency

One of the deepest harms done to our children in modern schooling is the treatment of difference as deficiency. When a child learns in ways that do not match the dominant classroom model, the system often assumes something is wrong with the child rather than questioning the model itself. A reflective learner may be called slow. A learner who needs movement may be labeled disruptive. A learner who watches before speaking may be judged disengaged. A learner who needs meaning before memorization may be seen as resistant.

These judgments do not arise in a vacuum. They come from educational systems built around speed, standardization, verbal performance, fragmented tasks, and narrow measurements of success. In such systems, children are rewarded for quick answers, immediate compliance, and the ability to repeat information on demand. But many of our children are not oriented toward learning in this way. They may need time to observe, space to reflect, and a fuller sense of purpose before they can respond with confidence.

When schools fail to recognize this, they do more than misunderstand learning; they undermine it. They create false narratives about intelligence.

The Harm of Speed-Based Classrooms

Many classrooms are organized around pace rather than depth. Lessons move quickly. Responses are expected immediately.

Children are often interrupted before their thinking has had time to form. In these environments, speed is seen as evidence of competence, while careful reflection is seen as a weakness.

For many of our children, this is a profound mismatch. A child may know the answer but need time to gather the whole of it. They may be considering not only the surface response, but the context, the consequences, the relationships, and the truth of what is being asked. When that child is rushed, the result may be silence, anxiety, or withdrawal. Over time, the child may begin to believe they are incapable, when in fact they are processing more deeply than the classroom allows.

This is one of the tragedies of modern education. It often mistakes fast recall for understanding and overlooks the kind of learning that is careful, relational, and lasting.

Mislabeling, Misdiagnosis, and Educational Injury

Because our children are often educated in systems that do not understand them, they are vulnerable to mislabeling. A child who is imaginative, sensory-aware, physically active, spiritually attuned, or deeply observant may be described as inattentive, oppositional, delayed, or disordered. A child who becomes overwhelmed by clutter, noise, fluorescent lighting, excessive words, smells, or emotional tension may be treated as though they are failing to regulate themselves, when they may actually be responding to an environment that is hostile to their learning.

This does not mean every diagnosis is false or that every educational concern is a misunderstanding. But it does mean that schools have too often lacked the cultural and human understanding needed to distinguish between disability, distress, difference, and depth. When this distinction is ignored, children can be placed into categories that follow them for years, shaping how teachers see them, how peers treat them, and how they come to see themselves.

The injury is not only academic. It is emotional, social, and spiritual. A child who is repeatedly told, directly or indirectly, that their natural way of learning is wrong may begin to disconnect from their own gifts. At home, families often have to work daily to undo that emotional damage.

When Memorization Replaces Meaning

Another way schools misread our children is by assuming that memorization alone is learning. In many classrooms, success depends on retaining isolated facts, repeating them quickly, and demonstrating mastery through standardized forms of recall. But for many of our people, knowledge is not meant to be separated from meaning.

A child may struggle to memorize information that feels disconnected, abstract, or purposeless. Yet that same child may remember a story, a place, a lived experience, a rhythm, a relationship, a scent, or a lesson tied to responsibility for years. This is not an inconsistency. It is a different memory structure.

When schools value only one kind of remembering, they fail to recognize the intelligence in another. They may conclude that a child cannot learn when in fact the child learns through meaning rather than fragmentation.

The Cost to Identity and Confidence

When misunderstandings occur repeatedly, they shape identity. A child who is constantly corrected for how they think, move, respond, or perceive may begin to hide parts of themselves or lose their authenticity to survive school. They may stop asking questions. They may stop trusting their instincts. They may become quiet, resistant, anxious, or angry. Some may try to survive by reshaping themselves to fit the system, even to the point of cutting their long hair, echoing an old wound our people have carried since the boarding school era. Others may withdraw altogether.

This cost is rarely measured in test scores, yet it may be one of the most serious outcomes of all. Education should help a child come more fully into their gifts, not teach them to abandon those gifts in exchange for approval.

For our people, this issue reaches beyond the individual child. When generations of children are taught to distrust their own ways of knowing, communities lose confidence in forms of intelligence that have long sustained life, family, and responsibility. The damage becomes intergenerational.

What Schools Need to Understand

If schools are to serve our children well, they must begin with a different question. Instead of asking, "Why is this child not fitting the system?" they must ask, "What is this child showing us about how learning happens?"

That shift changes everything. It invites educators to see silence as thought, movement as engagement, observation as participation, and relational understanding as intelligence. It asks schools to make room for stories, demonstration, sensory learning, place-based experience, reflection, beauty, and purpose. It asks them to understand that not all children enter knowledge through the same door.

Our children do not need to be reduced to be taught. They need to be seen.

Toward Educational Healing

To misread a child is serious. To misread generations of children is a structural failure. Yet this failure can be challenged. When families, educators, and communities begin to name the mismatch honestly, they create the possibility of educational healing.

That healing begins by recognizing that our children are not broken versions of someone else's standard. They carry ways of learning that are coherent, human, and worthy of respect. The task is not to force them into smaller forms of intelligence, but to build educational spaces large enough to meet them.

The next section turns more directly to that work by examining what parents, teachers, and schools can do differently to support our children's learning strengths.

What Parents, Teachers, and Schools Can Do Differently

Beginning With Respect Instead of Correction

If our children are to be taught well, they must first be seen clearly. Too often, adults begin with correction rather than understanding. They notice when a child is not following the classroom norm and immediately try to fix it. But when a child learns through observation, movement, reflection, sensory awareness, or relationship, correction without understanding can be harmful.

A better beginning is respect. Respect asks what the child is showing before deciding what the child lacks. It asks how this child enters knowledge, what conditions help them feel safe, and what forms of teaching foster their intelligence. This shift may seem simple, but it changes the entire educational relationship.

For our people, respect has never been separate from learning. A child learns best when they feel that who they are is not under attack.

What Parents Can Do

Parents and family members are often the first to recognize when a child is being misunderstood. They may notice that the child is bright at home, deeply observant in nature, emotionally perceptive, imaginative in play, or highly capable when learning through story, demonstration, and lived experience. These strengths should be named often and protected carefully.

Parents can help by reminding children that needing time does not mean they are less intelligent. They can explain that some minds learn by first gathering the whole picture. They can create learning environments with less clutter, less pressure, and more rhythm. They can use storytelling, hands-on activities, outdoor experiences, music, and practical responsibilities as teaching tools.

They can also advocate within schools. This may include telling teachers that a child needs wait time before answering, learns better through demonstration, becomes overwhelmed by sensory overload, or responds more fully when lessons are tied to meaning. Families should not have to translate for their children within institutions, but they often do. That advocacy can make the difference between a child being mislabeled and a child being understood.

What Teachers Can Do

Teachers do not need to know everything about our people to teach with greater wisdom, but they do need humility. They need to understand that the dominant classroom model does not fit every child and that intelligence takes many forms that schools do not usually reward.

A teacher can begin by slowing down. Give children more time before expecting a response. Allow observation before performance. Use demonstration, modeling, and story, not only verbal instruction. Connect lessons to real life, place, responsibility, and relationship. Reduce unnecessary clutter and overstimulation where possible. Make room for movement, sensory engagement, and quiet reflection.

Teachers can also change what they praise. Instead of rewarding only speed and verbal confidence, they can recognize careful observation, thoughtful silence, depth of connection, creativity, and relational understanding. A child who notices patterns, asks meaningful questions, or shows responsibility toward others demonstrates intelligence, even if that intelligence does not appear in the most conventional form.

What Schools Can Do

Schools must move beyond the idea that fairness means treating every child the same. True fairness means creating conditions in which different kinds of learners can thrive. This requires structural change, not just individual kindness.

Schools can provide more place-based learning, outdoor education, storytelling, arts integration, and experiential teaching. They can train educators to distinguish between difference and deficiency. They can reduce overreliance on speed, constant testing, and narrow behavioral expectations. They can create classrooms where beauty, calm, rhythm, and purpose are part of the learning environment rather than afterthoughts.

Schools can also build stronger relationships with families and communities. Elders, parents, and cultural knowledge holders should not be treated as outside the educational process. They carry forms of knowledge that can help schools better understand children. When schools honor that relationship, they become more human places of learning.

Supporting the Whole Child

One of the most important changes adults can make is to stop dividing the child into disconnected parts. Our children do not arrive as minds only. They arrive with bodies, senses, emotions, memory, spirit, and relationships. When education addresses only one part of the child, it leaves the rest unsupported.

To support the whole child means asking deeper questions. Is this child overwhelmed by noise, smell, lighting, clutter, or pressure? Does this child need movement to think? Does this child remember through story, rhythm, image, or touch? Does this child need to understand the purpose before participating? Does this child learn best through relationships and trust?

These are not minor questions. They are central to whether learning can happen at all.

Restoring Confidence and Trust

Once a child has been misread, part of the work becomes restoration. Adults must help rebuild confidence where school has created shame. This means clearly and repeatedly naming the child's strengths, showing them that their way of learning has value, and helping them understand that difficulty in a mismatched environment does not define their intelligence.

Restoration also requires trust. Children must be allowed to trust what they notice, how they process, and what helps them learn. If they are always forced to override their own senses and instincts, they may become disconnected from the very capacities that make them wise.

For our people, restoring confidence is not only about academic success. It is about protecting the child's wholeness. That protection can foster greater creativity in our children and support deeper social and economic self-sufficiency as adults.

Toward a More Human Education

What parents, teachers, and schools can do differently is not mysterious. Much of it begins with listening, observing, slowing down, and valuing forms of intelligence that have too often been ignored. The challenge is not a lack of possibility. The challenge is whether educational systems are willing to become more human than they have been.

Our children do not need an education that trains them away from themselves. They need one that recognizes their gifts, strengthens their confidence, and teaches in ways that honor life, meaning, and relationship. With or without the support of the educational system, our people have made it a priority to help heal the damage done to our children.

The next section turns to a broader conclusion: what our people's learning styles reveal not only about Indigenous children, but also about the limitations of modern education itself.

What Our Children's Learning Reveals About Education Itself

The Problem Is Larger Than Our Children

By this point, a deeper truth should be clear. The problem is not only that our children have been misunderstood. It is also that modern education has been built around a narrow idea of intelligence and then treated that narrowness as universal. When children who learn through relationship, reflection, movement, sensory awareness, story, and purpose are treated as deficient, the failure does not belong to the children. It belongs to the system that cannot recognize the full range of human learning.

What has happened to our children reveals something larger about schooling itself. A system that rewards speed over depth, memorization over meaning, compliance over wisdom, and fragmentation over wholeness is not merely failing one group of children. It is revealing its own limitations.

What Our People Have Always Known

Long before modern institutions defined intelligence through testing and standardization, our people understood that learning is relational. A child learns through watching, listening, doing, feeling, remembering, and belonging. Knowledge is not separate from responsibility. It is not separate from land, family, beauty, spirit, or the Creator. It is part of life.

This understanding does not belong only to the past. It remains relevant now because it speaks to what many children need, even when schools have forgotten how to provide it. The fact that our children are often harmed by modern education does not prove that they are unprepared for learning. It may instead show that modern education has become too detached from life.

The Myth of One Right Way to Learn

One of the most damaging assumptions in schooling is that there is one proper path to knowledge. Sit still. Listen quickly. Respond immediately. Memorize the parts. Repeat the answer. Perform under pressure. This model may work for some children, but it should never have been mistaken for the only valid form of learning.

Our children's experiences expose that myth. They show that some learners need the whole before the part, meaning before memory, observation before performance, and trust before participation. They show that silence can hold thought, movement can support concentration, and sensory awareness can deepen understanding. They show that intelligence is not a single, narrow behavior performed on command.

When schools refuse to accept this, they do not defend excellence. They defend conformity.

Education Must Return to Life

If education is to become worthy of children, it must return to life. Learning is not a mechanical process of information transfer. It is a living exchange shaped by relationship, environment, meaning, and purpose.

This means classrooms must become more human. They must make room for beauty, rhythm, reflection, story, sensory experience, and connection to the living world. They must allow children to encounter knowledge in ways that engage body, mind, memory, and spirit together. They must stop treating land, family, and community as irrelevant to intelligence.

For our people, this is not a new theory. It is a continued truth.

A Message Beyond This Book

Although this book centers on the learning styles of Indigenous peoples of Turtle Island, its message reaches beyond one community. What helps many of our children may also help many others. A more relational, meaningful, and humane education would not lower standards. It would deepen them. It would ask not only whether a child can repeat information, but whether they understand, carry, and live it.

In this way, our children's experiences offer a gift to the wider world. They reveal that education need not remain trapped within narrow definitions of success. Another way is possible.

Our Children Carry Their Own Wisdom

This book has argued that our children are not slow because they are weak. They are often thorough because they are trying to understand more. They are not empty when they are quiet. They are not broken when they need movement, meaning, or sensory connection. They are not deficient because they learn through relationships and the whole.

If a system cannot recognize these truths, then the system must be questioned.

Our people have always found ways to protect, teach, restore, and strengthen our children, even when institutions failed to do so. That work continues. It continues in homes, in stories, in land-based memory, in patient guidance, in encouragement, and in the daily refusal to let children believe the lie that they are less than they are.

Closing Reflection

The future of education will not be healed by forcing more children into narrow molds. It will be healed when adults become willing to see children more truthfully. Our children's learning styles call for that truth. They call for an education rooted in life, meaning, relationship, and respect.

If this book contributes anything, let it contribute this: a clearer seeing of our children, a deeper honoring of our people, and a stronger commitment to forms of learning that do not separate knowledge from life.

From this place, the work can continue.

Appendix: "What Is Your Learning Style?"

This book often speaks about the many ways children gather, process, and carry knowledge. Not every child learns through the same doorway. Some learn best by hearing. Some by seeing. Some by touching, moving, doing, or experiencing something directly. Some need the whole picture before the parts make sense. Some need relationship, meaning, rhythm, or place before learning can take root.

The resource "What Is Your Learning Style?" is included with this book to help readers reflect more intentionally on those differences. It is meant to support parents, educators, caregivers, and learners in recognizing that difficulty in one setting does not always mean inability. Often, it means the teaching method does not match how a child receives knowledge.

Why This Matters

When adults understand how a child learns, they are better able to reduce frustration, build confidence, and create conditions that make learning more natural. A child who struggles with memorization may thrive through story. A child who seems distracted may actually need movement or sensory engagement. A quiet child may be deeply processing rather than failing to participate.

Understanding learning style is not about placing a child in a rigid category. It is about paying closer attention. It is about noticing patterns, strengths, preferences, and conditions that foster intelligence.

How to Use This Resource

Readers can use "What Is Your Learning Style?" as a reflective tool alongside this book. It may help them recognize whether a child learns best through visual, auditory, kinesthetic, relational, or holistic pathways. It may help them notice whether a child needs context and purpose before memorization, or understand why some children do better with movement, story, rhythm, or outdoor experience. It may also help readers recognize that silence, observation, and sensory awareness may be part of learning rather than signs of deficiency, and support more informed conversations between families and educators about what a child needs.

A Word of Caution

No test or tool should be treated as the final word on a child. Children are living beings, not fixed categories. Their learning methods may change over time, and many children learn through more than one mode at once. The purpose of this resource is not to limit a child, but to help adults see them more clearly.

In the Spirit of This Book

This resource belongs with the larger purpose of this work: to help name what has too often gone unrecognized, to support our children with greater understanding, and to remind readers that intelligence takes many forms. When learning is approached with respect, patience, and a sense of relationship, children are more likely to flourish in ways that are true to who they are.

Used in that spirit, "What Is Your Learning Style?" can become one more bridge between misunderstanding and recognition.

References and Source Notes

This book draws from published research, educational guidance, author-created materials, and lived family and community knowledge. It is written in a simple, book-friendly source-notes style rather than as a strictly academic bibliography.

A Note on Research and Underrepresentation

There is still very little published research that fully reflects the learning styles, ways of knowing, and lived educational realities of Indigenous peoples. Much of what has been carried, observed, and understood in our communities has remained in oral history, family memory, cultural continuity, and lived experience rather than in formal academic systems. This is not because the knowledge is lacking. It is because Indigenous people have been profoundly underrepresented, misrepresented, and too often excluded from the institutions that decide what counts as research.

That underrepresentation matters. It means that many truths about our children have not been adequately documented in books, journals, or educational policy, even though families and communities have known them for generations. It also means that the absence of research should never be mistaken for the absence of knowledge. In many cases, what has not been fully written down has still been carefully carried.

This is one reason this book is so important. It helps name what has too often gone unnamed, brings lived knowledge into clearer public view, and offers a needed response to the long neglect of Indigenous children's ways of learning.

Source Notes

The following materials informed the research, reflection, and educational framing of this book:

- **Cornel Pewewardy, article available through ERIC**: https://files.eric.ed.gov/fulltext/EJ858583.pdf
- **M. R. Harrington, *Religion and Ceremonies of the Lenape*, Archive.org page reference**: https://archive.org/details/religionceremoni00harr/page/248/mode/1up
- **Portland State University resource via PDXScholar**: https://pdxscholar.library.pdx.edu/cgi/viewcontent.cgi?article=1009&context=rri_facpubs

- **JSTOR article**:
  https://www.jstor.org/stable/24398583
- **Journal of American Indian Education home page**:
  https://jaie.asu.edu/home
- **Smithsonian National Museum of the American Indian, Native Knowledge 360°:**
  https://americanindian.si.edu/nk360/
- **Native Financial Cents, "Native Learning Styles"**:
  https://nfc.aises.org/native-learning-styles
- **University of Oklahoma outreach resource, "Be Aware of American Indian Learning Styles"**:
  https://outreach.ou.edu/Educational-Professional-Development/PreK-12-Education/EDUTAS/Comprehensive-Centers-Archive/Knowledgebases/American-Indian-Education-Knowledgebase/Be-Aware-of-American-Indian-Learning-Styles
- **University of Denver, "Native American Pedagogies"**:
  https://inclusive-teaching.du.edu/native-american-pedagogies
- **ERIC entry ED335175**:
  https://eric.ed.gov/?id=ED335175
- **"Different Learning Styles,"** ***Why and How of Culturally Responsive Teaching***:
  https://whyandhowcrt.wordpress.com/2019/02/26/different-learning-styles/
- **Tyrese Gould Jacinto,** ***"What Is Your Learning Style?"***
  Author-created educational resource:
  https://www.nativeadvancement.com/what-is-your-learning-style.html

Lived and Community-Grounded Knowledge

This book also draws from lived family experience, long observation across generations, oral history, and community-grounded understanding. These sources are not secondary to the written materials. They are part of the book's foundation and are essential to its purpose, method, and truth.

Final Note

These source notes are intended to help readers understand the book's foundation in a clear, accessible way. If a more formal academic citation style is needed later, these materials can be expanded into a full bibliography.

Copyright and Publishing Notes

Authorial and Cultural Integrity

This work reflects a combination of research, lived experience, family knowledge, and long observation. It was written to support greater understanding of Indigenous children's ways of learning and to challenge patterns of misunderstanding that have persisted in educational systems.

Care has been taken to speak with respect, clarity, and responsibility. Some cultural knowledge remains private by necessity. Not everything carried by a people is meant for public explanation, publication, or institutional analysis. For that reason, this book shares what is appropriate for public learning while honoring the boundaries of what should remain protected.

Educational Use

Educators, parents, caregivers, and community readers are encouraged to use this book for reflection, discussion, and learning. If portions of this work are quoted, cited, or referenced in workshops, classrooms, articles, or presentations, proper attribution should be given to the author.

Permissions

Requests for permissions, excerpt use, classroom reproduction beyond fair use, translation, or republication should be directed to the author or the author's designated publishing contact.

Final Publication Details

About the Author

Tyrese Gould Jacinto

A Bright Flower Who Shares Wisdom With Children

Tyrese Gould Jacinto is an Indigenous author, artist, educator, and cultural advocate whose work is rooted in lived experience, spiritual understanding, and a deep commitment to the well-being of children. Through her writing, she seeks to help readers recognize the intelligence, sensitivity, and humanity that are too often overlooked in modern education systems.

Raised within a local Indigenous family, Tyrese brings together family knowledge, long observation, and a life shaped by relationship to land, community, and the Creator. Her work reflects a belief that learning is not separate from meaning, responsibility, beauty, or belonging. Across her books and public work, she continues to affirm the living presence of Indigenous people and the wisdom carried by children, families, and ancestral ways of knowing.

In addition to writing, Tyrese is an artist, herbalist, conservationist, and steward of the land. Her life's work has included cultural preservation, environmental care, community service, and the creation of books and teachings that bridge memory, healing, and practical understanding.

The Wisdom Our Children Carry grows from that lifelong commitment. It is part of her ongoing effort to help children be seen more clearly, to support families and educators, and to honor forms of learning that remain deeply human, relational, and whole.

Written and published by Tyrese Gould Jacinto

ISBN: 978-1-969075-22-3

Imprint: Independently published

Closing Note

This book is offered in a spirit of truth, care, continuity, and responsibility. Its purpose is not only to inform but also to help restore recognition where it has too often been withheld.

www.ingramcontent.com/pod-product-compliance
Lightning Source LLC
LaVergne TN
LVHW010841120826
845149LV00020B/3454
9781969075223